Background Artiste

A Play

Stephen Smith

A Samuel French Acting Edition

FOUNDED 1830

SAMUELFRENCH-LONDON.CO.UK
SAMUELFRENCH.COM

Copyright © 2000 by Stephen Smith
All Rights Reserved

BACKGROUND ARTISTE is fully protected under the copyright laws of the British Commonwealth, including Canada, the United States of America, and all other countries of the Copyright Union. All rights, including professional and amateur stage productions, recitation, lecturing, public reading, motion picture, radio broadcasting, television and the rights of translation into foreign languages are strictly reserved.

ISBN 978-0-573-12044-2

www.samuelfrench-london.co.uk

www.samuelfrench.com

For Amateur Production Enquiries

United Kingdom and World excluding North America

plays@SamuelFrench-London.co.uk

020 7255 4302/01

Each title is subject to availability from Samuel French,

depending upon country of performance.

CAUTION: Professional and amateur producers are hereby warned that *BACKGROUND ARTISTE* is subject to a licensing fee. Publication of this play does not imply availability for performance. Both amateurs and professionals considering a production are strongly advised to apply to the appropriate agent before starting rehearsals, advertising, or booking a theatre. A licensing fee must be paid whether the title is presented for charity or gain and whether or not admission is charged.

The professional rights in this play are controlled by Samuel French Ltd, 52 Fitzroy Street, London, W1T 5JR.

No one shall make any changes in this title for the purpose of production. No part of this book may be reproduced, stored in a retrieval system, or transmitted in any form, by any means, now known or yet to be invented, including mechanical, electronic, photocopying, recording, videotaping, or otherwise, without the prior written permission of the publisher. No one shall upload this title, or part of this title, to any social media websites.

The right of Stephen Smith to be identified as author of this work has been asserted by him in accordance with Section 77 of the Copyright, Designs and Patents Act 1988

BACKGROUND ARTISTE

First performed by Waterbeach Community Players at the Sawston Drama Festival on March 26th 1999 with the following cast:

Alf	Chris Shinn
Jessica	Sally Burgen
Mary	Jane Butcher
Enid	Bernardine Orrock
Walter	John Orrock

Produced and directed by Stephen Smith
Designed by Mark Easterfield
Stage Managed by Julie Petrucci
With the assistance of Martin Andrus, Simon Molloy, Valmai Furness and Roy Furness

CHARACTERS

Alf, middle-aged
Jessica, early 20s
Mary, thirties
Enid, elderly
Walter, elderly

The action takes place in the offices of a background artiste agency

Time—the present

Other plays by Stephen Smith published by
Samuel French Ltd

Departure
One-sided Triangle
Parentcraft

BACKGROUND ARTISTE

The offices of Alfredo Leache Artistes in London on a December morning

Alfred's desk, UR, *is littered with various papers and files. On the desk is a telephone and under the telephone is a* Yellow Pages *directory. In front of the desk is a chair for Alfred's clients.* UC *is Jessica's desk, equally untidy. On the desk, amongst the clutter, there is a telephone; a note pad and pen; a* Cosmopolitan *magazine and various directories, files and desk diaries.* DL *is a small coffee table with three chairs around it. On the table there are back copies of* The Stage *newspaper. Against the back wall* C, *there is a filing cabinet and some boxes. On the back wall* R, *there is a large display of photos of all the actors the agency represents and* L, *there is a noticeboard with theatrical posters and newspaper cuttings on it. All entrances and exits are made through the door* L

When the CURTAIN *rises, Walter and Enid are sitting at the coffee table. They are an elderly couple. Enid is wearing a pink hat, pink shawl and pink trousers. She is eating, with chopsticks, a Chinese take-away meal. Beside her chair is a large bag. Walter is wearing a raincoat and scarf. His left foot is heavily bandaged. He is reading a copy of* The Stage

Alfred Leach is sitting at his desk, and is on a telephone call to one of his clients. He is a middle-aged man and is dressed in black trousers with red braces, a shirt and a colourful tie

Alfred *(into the phone)* Yes love. ... Yes love. ... Yeah I quite understand, sweetheart, but isn't that what acting's all about:

become the character, live its life through you, use every fault and imperfection as a tool to assault the injustice of life. ... I know, I know, believe me, sugarplum, I've been there, but deep down, you know as well as I do, not all ducks are pretty. ...

Mary enters and walks up to Alfred's desk. She is casually dressed in a coat and carries a handbag. She is in her thirties

Let's face it, giving birth is embarrassing but we all have to do it!

Jessica, Alfred's secretary, enters and races up to Mary. Jessica is in her early twenties, smartly dressed and is wearing heavy make-up. She dreams of being an air stewardess and loves showing people to their seats. However, she looks like the kind of girl who works behind a perfume counter. She is a perfect vision until she opens her mouth

Jessica (*pulling Mary c, away from Alfred*) You're early. Alfredo's in a business meeting at present.
Mary Found you quicker than I thought.
Alfred (*looking at Mary; into the phone*) Would a bigger bottom help?
Jessica Excuse me for not smiling but I'm on a smile diet.
Mary Pardon?
Jessica (*picking up the notepad and pen from her desk*) Only close friends and family plus one new acquaintance a week, as it's only Monday I'd have nothing left to look forward to if I went for it now.
Alfred (*smiling at Mary; into the phone*) Perhaps smaller eggs then?
Jessica I hope you understand.
Mary (*unsure*) I think so.
Jessica Good. Every four thousand produce a wrinkle according to my flat mate so we've invested in a facial pension. Above our beds we have a sign, "Abstinence makes the face grow tauter". If you'd like to take a seat next to Enid and Walter ... (*She ushers Mary to her seat*)

Background Artiste

Mary Er... thank you. (*She takes off her coat and hangs it on the back of her chair*)
Jessica (*holding her notepad as if she is a waitress*) Drink?
Mary Yes please.
Alfred (*looking at Mary; into the phone*) Anyway it's the ugly ones people remember. ...

Mary's attention fixes on Alfred's telephone conversation

Jessica Tea or coffee?

Mary doesn't respond

Alfred (*into the phone*) Look at Orville or Vera Duckworth. ...
Jessica (*sternly*) Tea or coffee?
Mary Er — sorry — coffee please.

Jessica writes all Mary's answers on her pad

Alfred (*into the phone*) Even the ugly duckling himself. ...
Jessica White or black?
Alfred (*into the phone*) Look what happened to him, turned into a beautiful swan and went into ballet. ...
Mary White.
Alfred (*into the phone*) Precious, I had to pull a lot of strings to have a duck in "Snow White and the Seven Dwarfs", so let's not ruffle any feathers please. ...
Jessica Skimmed, semi-skimmed or full cream?
Mary Full cream.
Alfred (*into the phone*) Two months work is not to be sneezed at. Even if you are dressed as a duck with a crooked beak and an arse too tight to get your eggs through. ...
Jessica Sugar?
Mary Two please.
Alfred (*into the phone*) I'll tell you this much, if you had a crooked beak and a tight arse in real life you wouldn't need to do panto. ...
Jessica Demerara, granulated or Canderel?

Mary Granulated.
Alfred (*into the phone*) I could get you touring the Gulf states for ten times what the Alhambra are paying. ...
Jessica (*looking at Mary*) Not watching your figure?
Mary Canderel then.
Alfred (*into the phone*) All right, all right, I'll ring Bernie. (*He replaces the receiver*) God preserve us, I've got two ends of a pantomime horse that won't speak to each other, a goose with stage-fright and now a duck that refuses to lay eggs. Jessica, get me Bernie.
Jessica (*to Mary*) Be back in a minute. (*She moves to her desk and looks up the telephone number in one of the directories*)
Enid (*to Mary*) Eat what you like, dear. I do. (*She offers Mary a noodle*) Like some of this? I've got some spare chopsticks somewhere. (*She rummages around in her bag beside the chair*)
Mary No, thanks, I've just eaten on the train up here.
Enid That doesn't count as food though, does it?
Mary No, I suppose not.
Enid Can't beat Mr Hong's noodles.
Mary That's the Chinese take-away downstairs?
Enid As long as Alf keeps paying the rent we get the left-overs. I'll eat anything, me. Walter's much more fussy. Aren't you, love? (*She elbows Walter*)

Walter grunts from behind his newspaper

Given up eating it entirely now he's heard Mr Hong indulges in Shiatsu. Can't convince him it's a Japanese healing art, not an ingredient. Still he only used to muck about with it. Doesn't it irritate you, when you see them, out of the corner of your eye, playing with their pork balls.
Mary (*with politeness, but with wonder at what she has let herself in for*) Yes.
Enid Anyway a shapely body's not important in this game.
Mary Isn't it?
Enid No, got to look like the general public. That's the only qualification needed.

Mary I see.
Enid Bulk of the population are fat. That's why they're called the bulk of the population.

Jessica finds the number she has been looking for, and dials

As Jessica dials the number, Alfred's telephone rings

Alfred answers the phone. During the following telephone conversation, every time Alfred breaks to speak to Jessica he covers the receiver with one hand

Alfred (*into the phone; with a posh voice*) Alfredo Leache Artistes, Alfredo speaking. ... Dirk Van Dyke, yes he's one of our young, up and coming stable of nouveau riche actors. ... (*To Jessica*) Jessica, what's Dirk up for?
Jessica (*to Alfred*) Some Andrew Lloyd Webber. (*Into the phone*) Bernie please.
Alfred (*into the phone*) "Corpse Grinders". Yes, he was in that. Quite a meaty part if I recall. ... (*To Jessica*) Which one?
Jessica (*to Alfred*) Can't remember, either *Phantom* or *Cats*. (*Into the phone*) Alfred Leach Artistes.
Alfred (*to Jessica*) Alfredo Leache, how many times do I have to tell you Jessica? Let's have a bit of class. (*Into the phone*) That's right, shoved through the grinder and came out the other end into a bucket. Captures the full horror in not only a chilling disfigured way but with a hint of feline poetry. ...
Jessica (*to Alfred*) Put me on hold.
Alfred (*to Jessica*) Wouldn't have put you on hold if it'd been Sigourney Weaver playing the duck. Still I think I've got both bases covered here.
Jessica (*smiling to herself*) I'll hold for a minute, I like this tune.
Alfred Just find out which one it is, I can't bluff for ever.
Jessica I know what it is.
Alfred What? (*He grabs a pen to write it down*)
Jessica "The Wind Beneath My Wings" by Dolly Parton.
Alfred No, what Lloyd Webber musical Dirk is up for!

Jessica Oh right. (*She takes a big desk diary and starts to look through it*)

Alfred (*into the phone*) Did all his own stunts. When the cat knocked him off the chandelier it was all Dirk. Can play the full range from disfigured to dismembered with or without fur. (*Whispering to Jessica*) Found it yet?

Jessica (*studying the contents of the diary*) It's at the Apollo. I've got, Dirk see Apollo, written in here. Unless he's got a friend called Apollo. Does mix with a lot of Greek people.

Alfred What's on at the Apollo?

Jessica Although the see's only got one "e" in it. My spelling, I'd be embarrassed if I didn't know myself so well.

Alfred (*into the phone*) Sing? If so, I imagine falsetto. Dirk is one of our finest method actors, no doubt spent several hours soaking up the ambience of a meat processing factory. Unfortunately my *déjà vu* is not all it should be, so I'll have to check with a colleague who is more *au fait* with his résumé on this genre.

Jessica I've just remembered it's not "see Apollo", it's S.E. Apollo.

Alfred (*to Jessica*) Just hand me the file before he hangs up.

Jessica finds a rather empty file from her desk and without getting up, she holds out the file to Alfred

Jessica S.E. stands for something but I can't remember what.

Alfred stands

Alfred (*going to Jessica's desk to fetch the file*) Senile Elephant perhaps.

Jessica No, that's not it.

Alfred returns to his seat

Alfred (*into the phone*) Just been handed his file, Adrian, and what a weighty one it is. (*He opens the file to find just one sheet of paper*)

Jessica (*into the phone*) If you could. Alfredo Leache. Yes, from Alfred Leach Artistes. (*She replaces the receiver*) Going to ring back.

Alfred Dirk doesn't seem to have had the opportunity to flex his larynx in this one, Adrian, however I'm sure he's twanged his tonsils elsewhere. Just give me a few seconds to scan his curriculum vitae. ... (*His face drops*) Skate? ... (*He stares at Jessica*)

Jessica I know, don't tell me, S. E. is *Starlight Express*; isn't it? Slight problem with spelling so I thought best to abbreviate. Bit like putting something in a safe place and then forgetting where the safe place was. (*She stands and hurriedly goes to Mary with her pad*)

Alfred (*through gritted teeth; into the phone*) Right then Adrian, let's see what Dirk's done that could be relevant to *Starlight Express*.

Jessica (*looking at her pad*) Now it's one full cream coffee with two Canderel.

Mary Yes.

Jessica Plastic cup or mug?

Alfred (*frantically thinking of credits to enhance to Dirk's CV*) Er...

Mary Mug.

Alfred (*into phone*) Mug... "Mugged at Tooting Broadway". Had a small song and dance number in that one.

Jessica Biscuits?

Alfred (*into the phone*) "Garibaldi the Tank Engine." Little known Italian film.

Mary (*with exasperation*) No.

Jessica (*with shock*) No.

Alfred (*into the phone*) No... No, no communication cord at birth. Avant-garde student film. ...

Jessica Never met anyone who didn't want biscuits.

Alfred (*into the phone*) "Digestive Confessions of a Figure Skater." Sex film; didn't have a very big part in that. ...

Mary (*with annoyance*) I'm watching my figure.

Jessica quickly exits to get the coffee

Alfred (*into the phone*) Skating is skating, isn't it? As long as you stay upright and get there, who's complaining whether it's blades or wheels. If you can ride a bike, you can ride a horse that's our motto.

Enid (*to Mary*) Works very hard for his actors.
Alfred (*into the phone*) Actors are selected for their pliability at A.L.A, so when's the call? ...
Enid (*to Mary*) Got to be seen trying or they'll go elsewhere and he'll lose his percentage of what work he can get them. Dirk Van Dyke could be the next Dick you know.
Alfred (*into the phone*) Know it well. Don't fear Dirk will be there in *vitro compos mentis* (*He replaces the receiver*) Jessica, where are the *Yellow Pages*? (*He briefly looks for the* Yellow Pages, *which are under his phone on the desk*)

As Alfred searches for the directory, Mary plucks up enough courage to move up to Alfred. But Alfred doesn't notice Mary

Alfred exits looking for Jessica

Mary is left standing looking at his desk and then at her watch

Mary (*moving to collect her coat*) I think it was a mistake coming here.
Enid (*getting up and going over to Mary*) Don't worry love, no-one expects you to compete with the anaesthetic young actresses that flounce through here. Although of course, these days they don't call it anaesthetic ...
Mary No.
Enid (*turning towards Walter*) What is it these days that young girls have beginning with "B" ?
Walter (*puts down his newspaper and thinks for a while*) Barbie, is it?
Enid No, you idiot.
Mary (*helpfully*) Bulimia nervosa.
Walter What?
Mary Bulimia nervosa.
Walter Used to collect their stamps when I was a kid. (*He continues to read the newspaper again*)
Enid Have to excuse my husband.

Mary Right.
Enid Trod on a cocktail stick. (*She points to the large bandage on Walter's foot*) Went straight in. Couldn't get it out. Next-door neighbour wheeled him to the doctors in a barrow. We don't have a car. He blames it all on Mr Hong.
Mary What, the fact you don't have a car?
Enid No, his accident. Ever since he refused Mr Hong's left-overs strange things have happened.
Mary Surely that's just coincidence.
Walter (*putting down his newspaper*) Used to be regular as clockwork, now I'm all over the place.
Enid If he'd been going to the bathroom at his normal time it would never have happened. I didn't drop it until after lunch, use them as toothpicks. Look, still got all my own teeth. (*She flashes her teeth at Mary*)
Mary (*moving away from Enid*) Very nice.
Walter Never used to go in the afternoon until I stopped eating Mr Hong's food.
Enid (*returning to her seat*) Spooky I call it.
Walter Well known fact, these people from the East have powers that would make the average layman stand up.
Mary Where exactly does Mr Hong come from?
Walter Bury St Edmunds.
Mary Oh.
Enid Too close to the sugar beet for comfort if you ask me.
Walter Well known fact, too much white stuff never did anyone any good.
Enid And there's all this horriblistic medicine they indulge in.
Walter Talking to carrots and turnips.
Enid Treat vegetables like people and it's but a short step.
Mary Pardon?
Enid To the supernatural.
Mary You mean there's voodoo in Bury St Edmunds?
Walter Possibly, if they've got an Indian restaurant.
Enid Acupuncture, that's what we're talking about.
Mary With cocktail sticks?

Enid In times of crisis improvise. The aggrieved person releases their own tensions to seek out the body of their aggressor. I read that in *TV Quick*.
Mary I don't really think that's what acupuncture is about.
Enid (*pointing to his foot*) How do you explain his sock then?
Mary His sock?
Enid Cut his sock off you know.
Mary Who did?
Enid The doctor. Gets injured and loses a sock on the same day; that's not coincidence in my book, that's premenstrual.
Walter Come far?
Mary Bournemouth.
Walter We saw Des O'Connor in Bournemouth.
Mary Was he good?
Walter He was just walking down the road.
Mary Oh.

Jessica enters carrying a mug of coffee. She sees that Mary is away from her seat and guides her back

Jessica (*placing the coffee in front of Mary on the table*) One full cream mugged coffee with two Canderel; hold the biscuits.
Mary (*picking up the coffee*) Thank you.
Jessica Despite your initial negative answer, biscuits will remain on permanent standby.
Mary Right.
Jessica (*trying to please*) Ready to wing their way into your mouth should the need arise.
Mary OK.
Jessica (*hopefully*) Do you think the need may arise?
Mary (*firmly*) No.
Jessica Right. (*She sadly walks to Alfred's desk and takes the Yellow Pages from under his phone. She starts to look at the book, perched on the corner of Alfred's desk*)
Walter Would you like to see it?
Mary What?

Background Artiste

Walter The cocktail stick.
Enid Keeps it as a souvenir.
Walter (*producing the cocktail stick*) Luckily it went straight in and didn't break. Was so embedded it took two doctors and a nurse to pull it out.
Enid Had to have a tenuous jab in case it went semetic.
Walter Nearest I'll ever get to appearing in *Casualty*.
Mary In an acting part you mean?
Enid Walk-on.
Mary (*laughing*) Or in your case, Hop-on.
Walter (*with hurt*) Not funny to tread on a cocktail stick, you know.
Mary (*apologetically*) Sorry, I'm sure it isn't.
Walter Have you ever done it?
Mary No.
Walter Can be very painful.
Enid Small pricks can be the most painful.
Mary Undoubtably. Take my ex-husband for instance.
Enid What did he prick himself on?
Mary Just about everything.
Enid Accident prone?
Mary No, he made sure of that.
Walter Ignore her, she's got a nose like an anteater.
Mary It's all right. I don't mind talking about my ex-husband.
Enid Any kids?
Mary No.
Enid At least that's one good thing then.
Mary I suppose.
Enid Is that why you're here? Because of your divorce?
Mary Partly. I started the business with my ex, he's bought me out so I've got a little money to spend some time looking around. This looked exciting so I thought why not give it a go. Don't want to put all my eggs in the same basket again.
Walter Good you've got money.
Mary Why?
Enid Couldn't make a living doing this.
Mary Oh well there's always "plan B".

Enid What's that?
Mary The Lottery.
Walter *(disapprovingly)* We don't do the Lottery.
Enid Don't believe in gambling.
Mary I do a couple of pounds a week. Got to be in it to win it.
Walter Got to be in it to lose it too.
Mary Yes, I suppose so.
Enid Don't see why we should give our money, so that some undertaker in Carlisle can win it. What's he going to do with it?
Walter Bury it most likely.

Alfred's telephone rings

Jessica *(answering Alfred's phone)* Alfredo Leache Artistes. ... I'll just get him for you. (*She shouts offstage*) Alf, it's Bernie for you.
Alfred *(off)* Won't be a minute.
Jessica *(into the phone)* He's on the loo, so I'll just put you on hold. (*She goes to sit at her own desk, taking the* Yellow Pages *with her*)
Enid *(whispering to Mary)* Shouldn't have refused biscuits.
Walter Best bit about coming here. Tea and biscuits.
Enid As well as a nice warm office.
Mary You just come here to get warm?
Enid Only in the winter.

Alfred rushes in still trying to get his braces up and goes to his desk

Jessica *(triumphantly)* Got him on hold. Two can play at that game.

Alfred sits down gingerly and picks up the phone

Alfred *(into the phone)* Bernie, it's about Daphne. ... Yes Daphne the disgruntled duck. ... Not very happy with her dressing room—does she have to share it with all the dwarfs?
Mary Doesn't Alfredo mind?
Enid No, says we brighten the office. That's why I always wear pink.

Background Artiste

Alfred (*into the phone*) Problem is she's rather tall and they keep looking up her dress. Everybody now calls her Peking Duck.

Enid And we stop customers sitting here waiting for Chinese meals which prevents all sorts of confusion.

Alfred (*into the phone*) They keep planting all sorts of things in her plumage and using her beak as a frisbee while she's a villager in Scene One. Came on last night with a no-entry sign sticking out of her bum, and a hare-lip.

Enid One bloke was waiting for his thirty nine with egg rice and nearly ended up in a remake of *Gone with the Wind*.

Alfred (*into the phone*) Can't she share a dressing room with Snow White, I'm sure Christopher Biggins won't mind. ... The thing is Bernie, if we treat her well we could be talking Mother Goose next year, she's very versatile, can do anything in feathers. ... Great, owe you one Bernie, must rush. ... (*Trying to finish the telephone conversation as quickly as possible*) No, must rush, Bernie.

Alfred rushes out hurriedly, slipping off his braces as he goes

Walter, Enid and Mary watch his exit

Walter Terrible having to break off midstream.
Enid All that sitting around doesn't help.
Mary Being in a sedentary position.
Enid (*embarrassed*) Married at sixteen so we don't really know about that sort of thing.
Walter Could be right though, kinky sex can upset your bowels.

Jessica leaves her desk, taking the Yellow Pages

Jessica (*moving towards the coffee table*) I suppose no-one knows any good roller skating rinks.
Enid Never tried it.
Walter Enid's not one for being flat on her back in a public place.
Jessica Don't even have to be good. Dirk won't know the difference.

Mary Sorry.

Jessica I shouldn't be doing this you know, not with my hospitality skills. Born to be an air stewardess I was. Flight attendant as they now call it, although I prefer stewardess. More feminine, attendant makes it sound as if you work in a lavatory. Travel the world dishing out tea, coffee and the occasional orange juice, that was my dream.

Mary You could still do it.

Jessica No they wouldn't have me. I told them, as I'd been captain of the school netball team, I'd have no problems with heights. But they wouldn't have me because — (*she leans close to Mary's ear*) I wasn't a virgin.

Mary What?

Jessica There was this question on the form asking had I been a virgin employee before and as I've had several previous employers I had to say no.

Enid At least it wasn't because you were too stupid then.

Jessica No they said I was very bright and breezy, but that may have been because of my song.

Mary (*with shock*) You sang at the interview?

Jessica Thought my entertaining skills might impress. Do this cabaret show at old people's homes called "A Song and a Gingernut".

Mary What did they say to that?

Jessica Said they had another appointment.

Mary Oh well, there are other airlines.

Jessica My flatmate said you need to be born in Birmingham to work for British Midland and only a special type of girl works for Air Lingus so I've rather given up. I now spend my days trying to find things in the *Yellow Pages*. (*She looks through the* Yellow Pages) You know I'm sure some of this stuff is in the wrong section. I mean reproduction furniture, surely that should be under beds. (*She returns to her desk*)

Enid Nothing's straightforward anymore. When I was a girl no-one talked about sedentary positions or reproduction furniture.

Mary (*trying to change the subject*) So you two are only here to decorate the office and ward off customers for the Chinese downstairs?

Enid For how much longer I don't know. Mr Hong's getting on.
Mary How old is he?
Enid Not sure. His wife told me he was born in the year of the donkey.
Walter Can't imagine Hong as a donkey.
Enid His wife should know.
Mary You just sit here all day?
Enid On standby too.
Walter But we like to sit down.
Mary For what?
Walter In case someone doesn't show up.
Mary And you've done a lot of filming?
Walter (*leaning towards Mary*) I'll give you a good tip about filming.
Mary (*with interest*) Yes.
Walter Something we've learnt over the years.
Mary Yes?
Walter Could come in handy when you're more experienced.
Mary Yes?
Walter Food's best at ITV.
Enid Definitely.
Walter Sometimes get as much as four choices.
Enid Vegetarian dishes too if you don't like carnival knowledge.
Walter Forget the roast turkey on *Birds of a Feather*, can't beat *Emmerdale* for a decent cottage pie.
Enid Not all good though. *Touch of Frost* was very disappointing.
Walter Not fresh.
Enid No.
Walter But we've learnt over the years to avoid the BBC if possible.
Enid We worked on *Are You Being Served?* and weren't. Which says everything doesn't it?
Walter *Last of the Summer Wine* was another.
Enid Not enough to go around.
Walter No. The title often gives away the standard of catering.
Enid *Bugs*.
Walter *The Untouchables*.

Enid *Men Behaving Badly.*
Walter Titles like that and we bring our own sandwiches.
Mary (*laughing*) I suppose *London's Burning* is always overcooked.
Enid Really, I hadn't heard that.
Walter Thought you hadn't done any filming?
Mary I haven't it's just...
Walter Still despite everything, had some good times.
Enid Great adventures.
Mary Meet anyone famous?

Enid and Walter look at each other

Walter }
Enid } (*together*) } Not really.
No.

Walter But had some great meals. All free.

Alfred enters

Alfred Found anything?
Jessica (*leafing through the* Yellow Pages) Well, after a long search the closest I've got is roller shutter door manufacturers. Amazing how many there are.
Alfred (*standing over her*) That's no bloody good, is it.
Jessica Or ——
Alfred What?
Jessica Road surface dressing contractors. Not so many of them. There again how many road surface fancy dress parties have you been to lately.
Alfred Jessica?
Jessica Yes.
Alfred Do you know what you're looking for?
Jessica Roller skating rinks.
Alfred Then why not try S for skating instead. (*He returns to his desk*)
Jessica Now that's a good idea, why didn't I think of that.

Alfred sits down gingerly at his desk

Alfred (*sorting through some paperwork*) Good look at your parents will answer that question.
Mary (*to Enid and Walter*) Am I wasting my time?
Walter If you think you're gonna make a living out of it.
Mary Forget it?
Walter Only ten per cent of actors earn big money and the rest range from surviving to bugger all. Extras come in between the bugger and the all.
Mary But it can be a sort of exciting paid hobby.
Enid Exciting?
Walter Could spend all day on location and not get used.
Enid Can't wear pink.
Walter Could get used and the scene gets cut.
Enid Could get cut and the scene gets used.
Walter Then you can wear pink.
Enid Can start as early as six in the morning.
Walter In the middle of winter with high heels and only a mini skirt on.
Enid Didn't like that one did you?
Walter No.
Enid Not that we want to put you off.
Mary No of course not.
Enid At least Alf's one of the few legit ones.
Walter Alf's bona fide.
Enid Because he doesn't eat properly. Ought to try this. I'm going to cadge some more. Sure you don't want any?
Mary No thanks.

Enid exits

Walter returns to his newspaper. Mary gets out a mirror from her handbag and smartens herself up

Jessica (*picking up the* Yellow Pages *and going to Alfred's desk*) Lot of skip hire. What is that exactly?
Alfred (*sarcastically*) It's when you get bored with hopscotch.

Jessica Really. You know I never realized how educational this was. Ugh...
Alfred What?
Jessica Skin merchants!
Alfred (*grabbing the* Yellow Pages) Give me the book, forget fingers do the walking, it's more mouth do the talking with you. Here we are: Skating Rinks. Rollerworld. Get Dirk to dial this number and book up as many hours as possible.
Jessica He always goes for a facial on a Monday afternoon.
Alfred Ring him tomorrow then. Just tell him I've got an audition lined up for *Starlight* in a week's time.
Jessica (*looking towards Mary*) Speaking of auditions ...
Alfred Oh yes, send her over.

Jessica collects, from her desk, Mary's file

Jessica (*going over to Mary*) He'll see you now.
Mary Thank you.

Jessica ushers Mary to Alfred's desk

Jessica (*handing Alfred the file*) Mary Cavendish.
Alfred (*getting up to shake hands with her*) Pleased to meet you Mary. Take a seat.

Just as Mary is about to sit down, Jessica adjusts the chair

Jessica exits

Mary finally sits down

Now down to business. (*He sits down and opens Mary's file. The file contains a letter and a set of passport photos*) The reason we asked you to attend our offices, is that it provides you with the opportunity of seeing our base and staff, whilst enabling us to meet you in person. The most important thing, of course, is that we can check you look like your photo. (*He holds the set of photos in various positions and studies them*)
Mary (*slightly nervously*) Right.

Alfred (*still studying the photos*) However in your case I was intrigued to see if someone could really look like this and live.
Mary Not very flattering I'm afraid.
Alfred No. (*He hands them back to her*)
Mary I never seem to be able to coordinate my eyes and mouth with the flash.
Alfred Quite. Mutant ninja turtle with radiation sickness was our first impression.
Mary I sat on my pen.
Alfred Always a logical explanation. Well, we'll come back to the subject of photos. Now measurements. (*He looks at Mary's letter*)
Mary Yes.
Alfred I trust these are all recent. No point in fibbing.
Mary No.
Alfred Not a beauty contest. These measurements will be supplied to the production company's wardrobe department.
Mary Right.
Alfred If the costume doesn't fit you won't get paid.
Mary OK.
Alfred Good. (*He finds a form on his desk and starts to fill it in*) Anything pierced?
Mary What?
Alfred Any part of your body pierced, besides your ears of course.
Mary (*with surprise*) No.
Alfred Haven't succumbed to the current craze of drilling holes in anything that wobbles then.
Mary No.
Alfred Had one girl pierce her nose to cover up an enormous zit and then couldn't get the ring out. Buggers up continuity.
Mary Right.
Alfred Not to mention historical accuracy.
Mary I can see that.
Alfred Nipples.
Mary Pardon.
Alfred Don't hang anything from them do you?
Mary Certainly not.

Alfred Good. You wouldn't believe it, but I've seen nipple rings big enough to pick up Channel Five. Told Alastair they didn't like that sort of thing for presenters on the Christian Channel but he wouldn't believe me.
Mary Rest assured I have not and will not have anything pierced.
Alfred Tattoos?
Mary No.
Alfred Unsightly blemishes?
Mary No!
Alfred Big warts?
Mary Of course not.
Alfred Deformities of any kind?
Mary No.
Alfred Pity.
Mary What?
Alfred Anything out of the ordinary can be a selling point. Particularly in the horror market. Right — any specialities.
Mary I can wiggle my ears.
Alfred Not quite what we were looking for. Ride or juggle?
Mary What sort of thing?
Alfred Motorbikes, horses ...
Mary No.
Alfred Good I always think that's rather dangerous and cruel. By the way, I'm Alfredo Leache to my clients; Alfred Leach to my artistes; Alf to my friends.
Mary And which am I?
Alfred Friend and artiste I hope, so the choice is yours.
Mary I wouldn't exactly call myself an artiste.
Alfred Of course you are my dear. Don't put yourself down. The way you walked across the office showed you have poise.
Mary Did it?
Alfred Trust me, I'm a professional.
Mary With lots of different names.
Alfred But the same heart. To be a professional in this business we all have to reinvent ourselves. To impress, to stand out from the crowd. Where would a pizza be without pepperoni, a kebab without chilli sauce, a doughnut without jam. In your face that's

what it's all about. Change the name, use a bit of foreign, then the world's your *crêpe suzette*. Besides Alf Leach doesn't have the same *je ne sais quoi*.
Mary But Leach to Lech is hardly an improvement.
Alfred It is from where I'm sitting. Now then —

Both the telephones ring

Alfred looks at the phone on Jessica's unoccupied desk. He picks up his phone

Jessica enters carrying a cream bun

Alfred looks at Jessica angrily as she tries to hide the fact she has been out to buy a cream bun

(*Into the phone*) Alfredo Leache Artistes. ...

Jessica returns to her desk. She takes her Cosmopolitan *magazine from her desk and quickly starts to eat the cream bun behind the copy. She manages to get most of the cream round her face*

(*Into the phone*) Reg, what can we do for you? ... Three nuns with leather habits, four girls in gymslips and a goat for Sunday morning, no problem. (*He replaces the receiver*) Jessica, ring the convent later, tell them we've got another Business Training film.
Jessica (*peering over the top of her magazine, with cream splattered over her face*) Usual rates?
Alfred Yeah — no, better make it three crates of red wine. (*To Mary*) Had a slight accident with the goat last time. Now where were we?
Mary You were saying why you changed your name.
Alfred Enough of me, it's you we're supposed to be talking about.
Mary Sorry, it's just I used to be in consultancy and can't kick the habit of trying to improve everything.
Alfred Don't. Whereas I have to stand out in a crowd, you have to become one. Background artistes are seen and not heard. No individual characterizations or dialogue except crowd noises.

That's the rules of the game. Now you haven't got any other photos I suppose. Something we can use.

Mary picks up her handbag and looks for a photograph

Mary Only this on holiday in Caister ——

Alfred (*quickly interupting to try to stop Mary from taking out the photograph*) No you don't seem to understand. I need a black and white ten-by-eight head and shoulders shot to go into the directory. Like these. (*He stands up and goes over to his gallery of actor's photos*) These are the actors I represent. This is the main side of my business. Background artistes is a rather new venture.

Mary (*with shock*) I've got to have a photo like one of those?

Alfred Exactly. A proper professional one, not by your granny. That is what gets you work. Producers only want you for what you look like, nothing more, nothing less.

Mary That's going to cost a lot, isn't it?

Alfred Nothing comes for free, love. Look— (*pointing to the first photo*) this is Dirk Van Dyke, our matinee idol. Done a lot of telly, did the pilot in *Emmerdale Farm*.

Mary (*getting up and looking at it*) He was in the first episode?

Alfred No, he was the pilot of the plane that crashed and wiped out the farm part. Been in all the soaps.

Mary Such as?

Alfred *Eldorado, Albion Market...*

Mary *Coronation Street*?

Alfred Everyone does *Coronation Street*, he doesn't want too much exposure. His speciality is cameo roles, makes a crucial impact for a few seconds to pump up a sagging story. That's a rare gift.

Mary What has he done I'd remember?

Alfred Countless things. Currently up for *Starlight Express*.

Mary But can't skate?

Alfred Won't get cast of course, but this business is all about being seen. Sir Andrew himself could be sitting in on the *Starlight* auditions.

Mary But what good's that if he can't skate?

Background Artiste

Alfred If he sees Dirk making a prat of himself he's bound to wonder how did this pillock get an audition. Once he asks for Dirk's CV he'll discover Dirk's other talents. A year later Dirk could be in the kickline of "Margaret Thatcher the Musical". Simple as that.
Mary (*unconvinced*) I see.
Alfred Of course, I'll have to convince him he won't need to wear the fishnet tights. But that's all part of my job. (*He points to a photograph of an actress on the display board*) This is Daphne Cartliage, our *femme fatale*. Currently starring in "Snow White and the Seven Dwarfs".
Mary As a duck.
Alfred Got to be very versatile to play a duck. Not any five-year-old can do it. Hoping to put her up for *Dr Dolittle*. Make a great pushmepullyou with attitude. (*He points to another photograph*) This is our veteran character actor M.K. Beds.
Mary What does the M.K. stand for?
Alfred Milton Keynes. Currently in the number two tour of *Having A Ball*. The play about four men in a vasectomy clinic. To be truthful, Milton is the least likely person to ever need a vasectomy, one critic wrote his appearance in a vasectomy clinic was tantamount to showing off. But it was either that or back to the catalogues doing Y-fronts.
Mary (*worriedly*) You're not expecting me to do this sort of thing?
Alfred No, I'm just showing you the shop window. That I'm not only the pepperoni on the pizza, but the pepperoni with a sprinkle of parsley. (*He points to another photograph*) This is Veronica Room, she had the lead a few years ago in "I Was a Teenager Bedwetter", unfortunately never got a general release: few art house showings but she gets a steady income on the surgical appliance circuit.
Mary So what would my name be?
Alfred No need to change your name, love.
Mary Good enough is it?
Alfred No-one's going to see it are they. Your job is to turn up on set when you're called; put on whatever clothes they give you; do what the third assistant director tells you and get your chit signed.

Mary But I have to pay to join?
Alfred To have a half-page in our brochure which we send out to all the film and television companies.
Mary How much is that?
Alfred Seventy-five pounds a year and then we charge thirteen per cent commission.
Mary And how much work can I expect?
Alfred Can't guarantee any, only that we will work extremely hard on your behalf to submit you for any production that you are suitable for.
Mary Oh.
Alfred (*starting to feel the urge to leave the office again*) However now I've seen that you're not like your photo, we'd very much like to have you aboard. So what do you say?
Mary Can I think about it?
Alfred Course you can, course you can ... Jessica will fill you in with all the details. I've just got to nip out for a minute.

Alfred rushes out

Mary goes to pick up her handbag

Jessica (*going up to Mary and ushering her back to her seat*) Do you want to read the terms and conditions?
Mary Please.
Jessica I'll go and get them.

Jessica moves to her desk

Mary (*moving to sit next to Walter*) How long have you been here?
Walter Since nine.
Mary No I meant how long have you been with the agency?
Walter We're not with the agency.
Mary You're not?

Jessica returns to Mary with the "Terms and Conditions"

Jessica (*sitting down next to Mary*) Here you are.
Mary Thank you.

Jessica Would you like me to read them for you?
Mary (*taking the "Terms and Conditions" from Jessica*) No, I can read, thank you.
Jessica Just thought I could go over all the points with you.
Mary I'll ask if there's something I don't understand.
Jessica (*disappointedly*) Right. (*She returns to her desk*)

Enid enters carrying some more food

Enid Beansprout anyone?
Mary No thanks.
Enid Spring roll?
Walter Wrong time of year.
Mary Walter just told me you're not with this agency.
Enid Not as such, no.
Mary How do you mean, not as such?
Enid We own it.
Mary What?
Enid Part of it, to be precise.

Enid and Walter now speak the following with well articulated and refined theatrical accents. This is in contrast to the earlier "down-market" character parts that they had each invented. Enid takes off her pink shawl and hat. Walter takes his raincoat and scarf off to reveal a jacket and cravat

Walter Alf's our son.
Enid We like to vet all the potential clients first. If I leave the room it's the thumbs up and if Walter leaves the room we think they should be sent to the vet.
Walter (*pointing to Mary's chair*) That's the R.I.P. chair.
Enid Reliable, interested and punctual. That's what we have to decide. Take the stars out of their eyes and see if they'll stick at it. We can't have people who jack it in after the first day of shooting because it's not what they expected.
Walter (*taking off his bandage*) Alf's a busy man. Don't want him wasting his time doing the spiel for no hopers. Been struggling to make ends meet with the legit actors so we decided to help him expand.

Mary I'm not very happy about this.
Walter Then don't join. This is a business in which everyone is going to be judging you at a superficial level. Nobody reads the book, they only look at the cover.
Mary So all this stuff before was an act?
Enid Getting too old to tour, this has to be our stage now.
Walter Much more money in this than doing rep.
Enid So we sunk our savings into Alf's business to create a background artistes agency.
Walter Whilst remaining in the background ourselves.
Enid Have we put you off or are you still interested?
Mary Made me realize it's not at all glamorous.
Walter If you want glamour, try ballroom dancing.

Jessica's telephone rings

Jessica (*answering the phone*) Alfred Leach Artistes.
Enid It's a part-time job and like all jobs has its ups and downs.
Jessica (*into the phone*) I'm afraid he's out of the office at the moment. ...
Walter Once you forget all the bogus stories about being discovered and becoming famous, you'll be able to enjoy it for what it is.
Enid And your friends and family might notice your six seconds in a lift, with someone out of *The Bill*.
Walter You'll spend ninety per cent of the time sitting around.
Enid But meet some interesting people from all walks of life.
Walter The stars will ignore you.
Enid But you'll soon realize that they are no better than you.
Walter Because they're just doing a job too.
Jessica (*into the phone*) Right I'll tell him. ... (*She replaces the receiver*)

As Jessica replaces the telephone receiver, Alfred enters

Alfred Who was that?
Jessica Bob. Says he's casting for *Star Trek, The Next Generation Game*.

Alfred What?
Jessica Apparently Bruce Forsyth's playing Captain Kirk.
Alfred He's got the wig for it.
Jessica Some sort of spoof sci-fi. Michael Caine's Sulu and Kate Moss is Bones.
Alfred Suppose they're looking for an Irish actor to pay Ohura.
Jessica How did you know that?
Alfred What did he want?
Jessica Mutants.
Alfred Really. (*He looks at Mary*)
Jessica Preferably female mutants, something to do with Spock's upbringing. Shall I get him back?
Alfred In a minute. (*He moves towards Mary*) Could I possibly see that photo again?
Enid Here's your chance.
Mary I still haven't decided.
Alfred If there's a part lined up, no need to pay to go into the directory for this one.
Mary No need to pay?
Alfred Only the commission. Then you can see how you feel if you want to go into the directory.
Mary All right, why not. (*She hands him the passport photos*)
Alfred Good. Jessica, get me Bob.

Jessica dials the number

No guarantees mind, but you've got nothing to lose, have you?
Mary Except my self-respect.
Alfred But it's not supposed to be you up there on the screen, is it?
Mary No, I suppose not.
Jessica (*waiting while the phone rings; to the others*) The thing that always puzzles me is how Chekhov managed to find time to do all that writing.
Walter Dodging all those Bolsheviks.
Jessica Yeah, they were even worse than the Klingons.
Mary She doesn't need to carry on with the act now, you know.
Enid Oh that's not an act, she really is like that.

Walter Makes you wonder what she thinks the Captain's log is.
Alfred (*to Jessica*) Have you got him?
Jessica (*into the phone*) Just putting you through.

Jessica transfers the call to Alfred's phone which rings. Alfred answers the phone

Alfred (*into the phone*) Bob, hear you're looking for mutants. Well, today's your lucky day, have I got a mutant for you. ...

Everyone turns to look at Mary, who looks decidedly uncomfortable

The CURTAIN *falls*

FURNITURE AND PROPERTY LIST

On stage: **Alfred**'s desk. *On it*: various papers, forms and files; pens; telephone; *Yellow Pages* directory. *Behind it*: office chair. *In front of it*: chair for clients
Jessica's desk. *On it*: telephone; note-pad and pen; *Cosmopolitan* magazine; various directories; desk diaries; file with one sheet of paper; file containing a letter and a set of passport photographs; the "Terms and Conditions" leaflet. *Behind desk*: office chair
Small coffee table. *On it*: back issues of *The Stage* newspaper
Four chairs around coffee table
Filing cabinet
Boxes
Large display of photos of actors on the back wall
Noticeboard. *On it*: theatrical posters and newspaper cuttings
Chinese meal with noodles; chopsticks for **Enid**
Large bag for **Enid**

Off stage: Handbag containing a mirror (**Mary**)
Mug of coffee (**Jessica**)
Cream bun (**Jessica**)
Chinese food (**Enid**)

Personal: **Walter**: bandage on foot; cocktail stick
Mary: watch

LIGHTING PLOT

Property fittings requried: Nil

To open: General interior lighting

No cues

EFFECTS PLOT

| Cue 1 | **Jessica** dials a number on her telephone
Alfred's *telephone rings* | (Page 5) |

| Cue 2 | **Walter:** " Bury it most likely."
Both telephones ring | (Page 12) |

| Cue 3 | **Alfred**: "Now then —"
Alfred's *telephone rings* | (Page 21) |

| Cue 4 | **Walter**: "...try ballroom dancing."
Jessica's *telephone rings* | (Page 26) |

| Cue 5 | **Jessica** transfers the call
Alfred's *telephone rings* | (Page 28) |

Lightning Source UK Ltd.
Milton Keynes UK
UKHW021534080522
402613UK00008B/447

9 780573 120442